THE GOOD GOLF GUIDE

CORRECTING
COMMON FAULTS

This material previously appeared in *Improve Your Golf*.
This volume compiled by Paul Foston and Sally Hiller.

CLB 3293
© Eaglemoss Publications Ltd 1989, 1990, 1991, 1992

This edition published in 1995 by SMITHMARK Publishers,
a division of U.S. Media Holdings, Inc.,
16 East 32nd Street, New York NY 10016

SMITHMARK books are available for bulk purchase for sales promotion and
premium use. For details write or call the manager of special sales,
SMITHMARK Publishers, Inc.
16 East 32nd Street, New York,
NY 10016; (212) 532-6600

Produced by CLB Publishing
Godalming Business Centre
Woolsack Way, Godalming, Surrey, UK

ISBN 0-8317-7478-9

Printed in Hong Kong
10 9 8 7 6 5 4 3 2 1

PICTURE CREDITS
Photographs: 9 Sporting Pictures UK, 27 Allsport/David Cannon,
67(t) Keith Hailey, 67(b) Phil Sheldon Photography
All other photographs: Eaglemoss/Phil Sheldon

Illustrations: 60-62 Kevin Jones
All other illustrations: Chris Perfect/ Egg Design

Cover: Below left: Peter Dazeley
All others: Eaglemoss Publications

THE GOOD GOLF GUIDE
CORRECTING
COMMON FAULTS

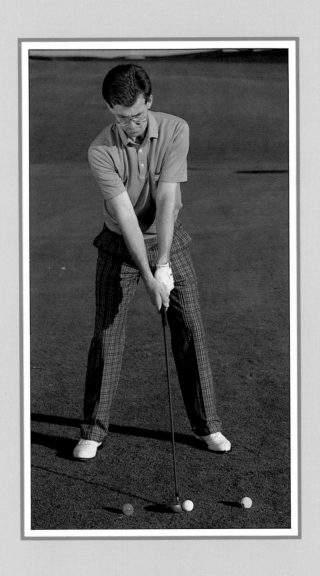

CONTENTS

INTRODUCTION

Imagine never miss-hitting or striking a ball off-line ever again. Wouldn't golf be fantastic if all your shots were perfect? This of course is impossible, but you can reduce the chance of a poor shot by increasing your knowledge of the golf swing.

You are only as good as your bad shots and everyone – weekend golfer as well as professional – hits them, but it is those who hit the fewest and the least destructive that post the best scores.

Correcting Common Faults takes you back to basics, then moves on to perfecting your balance, before taking a look at positioning of the body at impact. All world-class players are correct at the start of the swing and at the moment of impact, and you must strive to get into these positions if you are to achieve any degree of excellence. Finally, the book takes a look at swing path and swing plane, both of which are crucial to the shape of your shot.

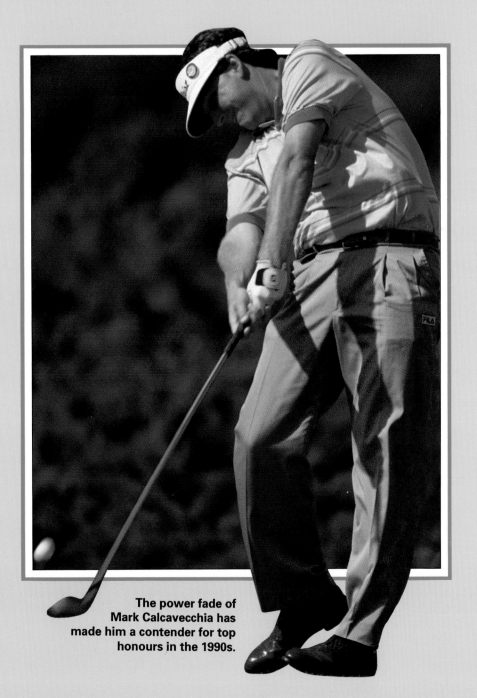

The power fade of Mark Calcavecchia has made him a contender for top honours in the 1990s.

BACK TO BASICS

It's all too easy to neglect the basics in your eagerness to play your shot. You need to develop a consistent and repeatable pre-shot routine that you can maintain under pressure. Your aim, grip, stance and posture must all be considered before you strike the ball. Remember: one good move leads to another.

Sandy Lyle takes up a relaxed position over the ball with a classic set-up. He is well balanced and his posture is superb. Notice how he keeps his chin up clear of his chest to allow the free passage of the left shoulder.

Grip problems

One of the most common faults in golf is a bad grip. Even with a perfect set-up and swing, the ball won't travel absolutely straight if your grip is wrong.

The function of the grip is to return the clubface square to the ball-to-target line at impact. Anything other than a perfect grip results in the ball travelling right or left of the target.

However experienced you are, you should frequently check the position of your hands on the club.

It's easy for a tiny error to creep into your grip without you realizing the change.

CHECK GRIP FIRST

Because most bad grips feel comfortable, many players attribute poor shots to a swing fault. They end up changing their set-up to try and cure the problem but this only makes matters worse – two wrongs don't make a right.

Whenever your game goes sour, start by checking your grip because most faults are caused by a basic error. Only if your grip is correct should you start checking other parts of your game, such as body alignment, stance and ball position. Remember that gripping the club correctly is the most important part of your game.

With the correct grip you see one and a half knuckles on your left hand, while the V between your right thumb and right forefinger points directly at your chin.

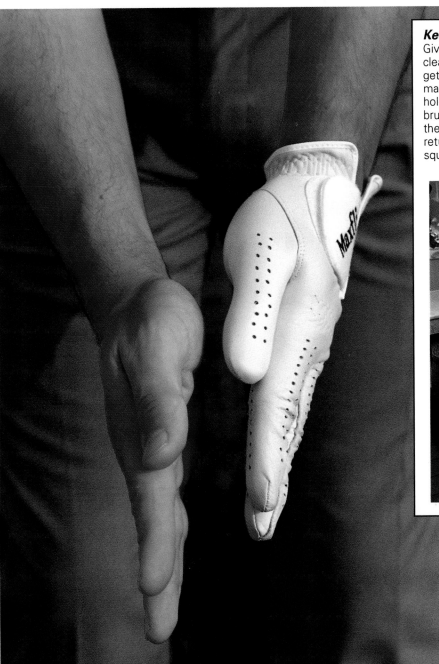

Keep them clean
Give your golf the best start by cleaning your grips regularly. Dirt gets trapped in the ridges of a grip, making it slippery and reducing your hold. Remove all the grime with a brush and soapy water and towel the grips dry. It's very difficult to return the clubface square to the ball if your hands slip.

HANDS SQUARE AT IMPACT
To feel the perfect impact position, take up an imaginary set-up, with your hands stretched out and square to the ball-to-target line. Your hands dictate the position of the clubface. At impact, the back of your left hand, the palm of your right hand and the clubface should be square to the ball-to-target line.

GOOD AND BAD GRIPS

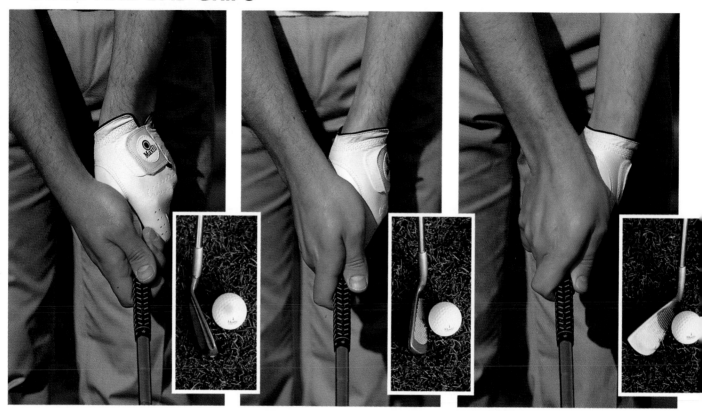

STRONG GRIP
At address you see more than one and a half knuckles on your left hand and the V on your right hand points right of your chin. The clubface is closed at impact, making the ball go left.

CORRECT GRIP
With a perfect grip you see one and a half knuckles on your left hand and the V on your right hand points at your chin. At impact the clubface is square and the ball flies straight.

WEAK GRIP
At address you see one or no knuckles on your left hand and the V on your right hand points left of your chin. The clubface is open at impact and so the ball flies right of the target.

STRONG GRIP

CLOSED CLUBFACE

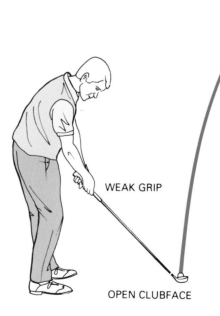

WEAK GRIP

OPEN CLUBFACE

HOOK OR PULL
With a strong grip your hands close the clubface at impact. The ball is hooked or pulled to the left. It's an easier fault than a weak grip to remedy.

SLICE OR PUSH
With a weak grip, your hands fail to square the clubface through impact. It remains open on the downswing and the ball is sliced or pushed to the right.

GETTING TO THE CORRECT GRIP

1

2

2 GRIP CLUB
Rest the club against the palm of your left hand. Place your left thumb down the shaft and wrap your fingers around it. Add your right hand to the grip – your thumb points down the shaft. The little finger of your right hand overlaps the forefinger of your left hand.

1 GET HANDS SQUARE
To get your hands square, adopt a set-up with arms stretched and hands open, your left slightly ahead of your right. At address the back of your left hand and the right palm should be square to a ball-to-target line.

pro tip

Strengthen your fingers
Squeeze a squash ball in the palm of each hand in turn. Repeat the exercise several times a day – strong fingers are an advantage in golf. They help you keep a firm grip of the club

and prevent it slipping in your hands.

If your fingers are weak it's difficult to square the clubhead through impact. The clubface stays open and the ball goes right.

With a bad grip your hands are too much to one side – how far varies. If your hands are too far right your grip is called strong; too far left is known as a weak grip. Strong or weak in this sense doesn't refer to how tightly you hold the club, but describes where your hands are placed on the grip.

THE STRONG GRIP

If you have a strong grip you see more than one and a half knuckles on your left hand and your right hand V points right of your chin.

With a strong grip, your hands automatically close the clubface at impact and the ball swerves to the left. The stronger your grip, the further right your hands – and the ball flies further left.

THE WEAK GRIP

When both your hands are left of the correct position, the V on your right hand points left of your chin and you see less than one knuckle on your left hand.

This prevents your hands naturally squaring the clubhead through impact. The clubface stays open, hitting the ball right of the target. The further left your hands are, the weaker your grip and the further right the ball goes.

A weak grip causes more prob-lems than a strong grip. Squaring the clubhead through impact is difficult at the best of times – even with the correct grip. A weak grip exaggerates the problem, resulting in a massive slice.

GRIP IT RIGHT

Spend time setting up the basics of a good standard overlap grip. Adopt a normal relaxed stance with your arms and hands stre-tched out. Set the back of your left hand and the palm of your right hand square to the ball-to-target line.

Keeping your left hand open, take the club firmly in your right hand and place the grip against the palm of your left hand.

Close the fingers of your left hand around the club, with your thumb pointing down the front of the shaft. Make sure there is about a 2in (5cm) gap between the butt (end of the shaft) and your left hand. You should see one and a half knuckles.

Add your right hand to the grip, so that your right thumb covers most of your left thumb and points left of centre down the shaft. Let your fingers wrap around the grip with the little finger of your right hand resting on the cleft between forefinger and middle finger of your left hand. Don't grip

the club too tightly. This is the standard overlap grip.

OLD HABITS DIE HARD

Curing a grip fault is harder than you think – particularly if how you hold the club differs greatly from the correct grip. Old habits die hard. It isn't easy to discard a bad grip that feels comfortable, even when you've identified it as the reason your shots travel off line.

The correct grip may feel un-natural at first. But don't be tempted to go back to your old one. Unless you persevere your problems remain.

You'll need lots of practice before you see an improvement. Don't expect your shots to get dramatically better overnight. And don't expect your grip to feel comfortable straight away.

Only through constant practice with a correct grip that seems strange to begin with does your new hand position start to feel natural and your shots improve.

The practice grip
This is moulded to place your hands and fingers exactly on the grip. If your grip is strong or weak, it helps you become accustomed to the correct grip. Fix a practice grip to an old club and use it regularly until the correct grip feels comfortable and you automatically take it up. But note that it's against the rules to use this aid in competition.

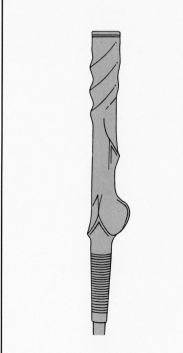

Alignment faults

Aligning your body correctly is one of the most vital basics in golf. You swing around your body, so if you're facing in the wrong direction you're unlikely to swing along the proper path.

DEVELOPING A FAULT

To make up for misalignment, your body devises a compensating movement – a fault – to bring the club along the path you want. Although this may work to begin with, your consistency is bound to suffer eventually. By then, the fault has become ingrained in your swing and is much harder to erase.

Make sure you're aligned correctly, so that you can build an orthodox swing. The body – your feet, hips and shoulders – is properly aligned when parallel to

ARE YOU PARALLEL?
Correct alignment is vital for a proper swing path and smooth body rotation. Use clubs on the practice ground to check your shoulder, hip and feet alignment at address.

Shoulder out of sight
When you're on the course, a simple way of checking alignment is to look at the target and make sure you can't see your left shoulder.

Correctly aligned, your left shoulder should be only just out of sight of your left eye. If you can see it, you're almost certainly aligned right of target.

HOW POOR ALIGNMENT CAUSES BAD SHOTS

WRONG – ALIGNING LEFT
A slice can result from aligning yourself too far to the left. You're no longer parallel to the ball-to-target line – your backswing becomes severely restricted because you can't make a full shoulder turn at 90° to your ball-to-target line. This causes you to tilt rather than turn your shoulders. An out-to-in swing path results, making a slice very likely if the clubface is open at impact. Should you close the clubface at impact you pull the ball – it flies immediately left.

 It's worth remembering that slicing and pulling are the most common bad shots in golf. At least half the time the root cause is poor alignment.

WRONG – ALIGNING RIGHT
If you align too far to the right of the ball-to-target line, you swing from in to out. This creates too much spin as the club swings across – rather than through – the ball. When the clubface is closed a hook results, while an open clubface causes a push – the ball flies straight to the right.

 A slice can also occur, especially with less experienced players. You subconsciously realize at the top of the backswing that you're wrongly aligned and try to adjust. This last minute change causes you to swing from out to in, as you try to pull the club around your body. With a closed clubface in this situation you pull the ball – if it stays open you slice.

the ball-to-target line.

The body should face slightly left of target (right of target for left handers). This lets you swing the club easily towards the target without obstruction by your body. Never make the mistake of trying to align your body directly at the target – golf is not like rifle shooting and the clubhead is not as close to your body as a rifle is.

SHOULDERS, HIPS AND FEET

The order of importance in your alignment is shoulders, hips and feet. Your shoulder alignment is crucial because the shoulders begin your body turn. Many players neglect the shoulders in favour of the feet because they can clearly gauge feet position but can't see their shoulders.

Remember that your whole body – for which your shoulder, hips and feet are the check – must be properly aligned, after you've aimed the clubface. You can't swing well if one part is correct and another is wrong. Poor alignment ruins good body turn.

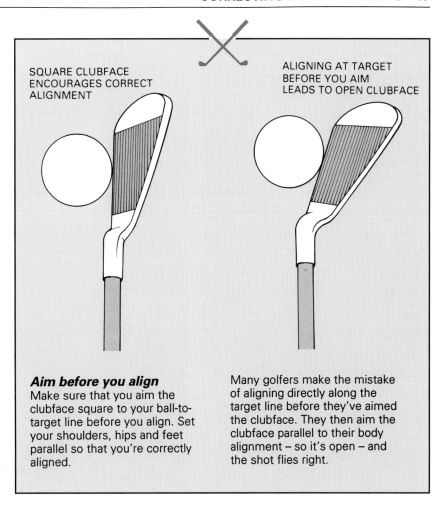

SQUARE CLUBFACE ENCOURAGES CORRECT ALIGNMENT

ALIGNING AT TARGET BEFORE YOU AIM LEADS TO OPEN CLUBFACE

Aim before you align
Make sure that you aim the clubface square to your ball-to-target line before you align. Set your shoulders, hips and feet parallel so that you're correctly aligned.

Many golfers make the mistake of aligning directly along the target line before they've aimed the clubface. They then aim the clubface parallel to their body alignment – so it's open – and the shot flies right.

GOOD ALIGNMENT

CORRECT – ALIGNING SQUARE
Your body is correctly aligned when your shoulders, feet and hips are parallel to the ball-to-target line. Only then can you swing along the correct path and let your body complete its proper turn.

pro tip

Check your alignment

When you're on the practice ground, always pick a target at which to aim. Many players simply whack balls without considering where they want them to fly.

Once you've chosen a target, picture a line running from it through the middle of the ball.

Check the alignment of your upper body to that line by holding your club lengthways across your shoulders and chest. Then lower the club and lay it along the ground just in front of your feet. Does it run parallel to your ball-to-target line? If it does, your alignment must be correct.

Although you can't carry out this procedure on the course, it's an effective practice ground routine. Many top pros use it, as you'll see if you spend some time watching on the practice ground at a tournament.

HOOKING AND PUSHING

ADDRESS
From a closed stance – when your body is aligned right – you're likely to hook or push the shot.

BACKSWING
You tend to swing the club inside the line early in the backswing causing an in-to-out path.

IMPACT ZONE
The in-to-out path causes a hook if the clubface is closed at impact or a push if the face is open.

Check your ball position

Placing the ball correctly is one of the most neglected fundamentals in golf. When they play a wayward shot, many players analyse their swings in search of the cause – but faulty ball position could be the culprit.

Being out of place by as little as a ball's width can make all the difference between striking off the heel, toe or sweet spot of the club.

It's all too easy to take your stance so that the ball is too far back or forward – so quickly check where the ball is every time.

STANCE WIDTH

You must strive to use the same swing for all 13 lofted clubs – apart from helping your tempo, it's much easier than having 13 different swings.

To repeat your swing throughout the bag, adjust your ball position and stance width as the club length changes. Your purpose is to hit the ball on the lowest part of your swing with every club – except the woods, which you need to hit on the upswing.

For example, with the long clubs – such as your driver – the ball should be opposite your left heel. It moves nearer your feet and towards the middle of your stance as club length lessens. With the medium irons, the ball is between the centre of your stance and your left heel. With the short irons the ball is central.

Change your stance so that it's widest with the driver and narrowest with the heavily lofted clubs.

PATH AND PLANE

To understand completely the importance of correct ball position it's vital to recognize the part played by swing path and swing plane.

The plane is the angle of your swing path in relation to the ground. It's judged by two things – your height and the distance

PERFECT PLACING
The ball should always be between two points – opposite your left heel and the centre of your stance. This position differs from driver to short iron. Because the face of each club is square to the ball-to-target line only for a split second, it's vital that you set up with the ball in the correct spot.

BALL POSITION – DRIVER

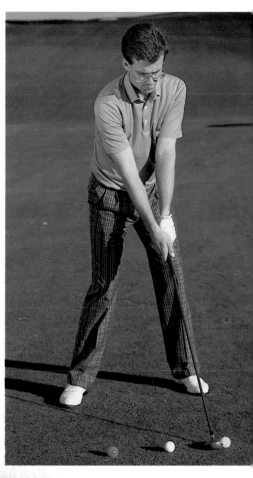

BALL TOO FAR FORWARD
You're likely to hit the ball left, because at impact the clubface is closed and your upper body is open. You may also hit the ball thin (halfway up) because the clubhead makes contact too high on the upswing. The ball probably scuttles along the ground with little power or distance.
▶ The white ball is correctly placed opposite the left heel.

WHERE DO YOU PLACE THE BALL?

With the longest clubs – for which you take your widest stance and place the ball furthest away from you – the ideal position for the ball is opposite your left heel. Move the ball nearer the centre of your stance – bringing your feet closer together – as club length shortens. The ball should be in the middle of your narrowest stance with the short irons. A normal stance must be square on to the ball-to-target line.

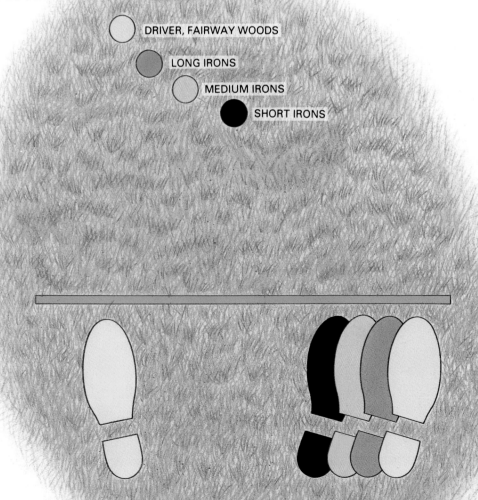

DRIVER, FAIRWAY WOODS
LONG IRONS
MEDIUM IRONS
SHORT IRONS

BALL TOO FAR BACK
You hit immediately right because the clubface is open at impact and your upper body is closed. You may strike the ball fat (behind), because the clubhead has not yet reached its lowest point in the swing, and meets the ball too soon. **✗**

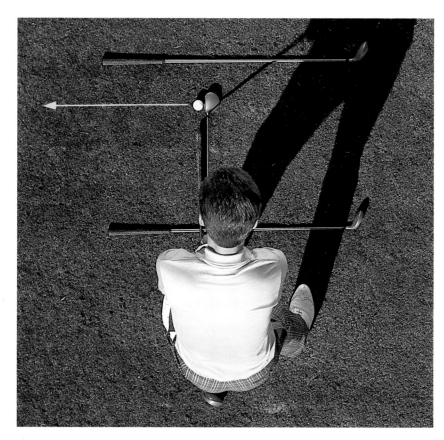

CORRECT – OPPOSITE LEFT HEEL
The proper ball position for a driver is opposite your left heel. You make contact the moment the clubhead begins to rise – which helps the ball gain height – and during the split second when the clubface is square to the target line. **✓**

SET YOUR POSITION: SHORT IRONS

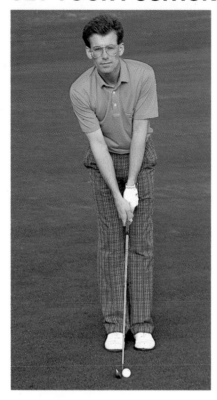

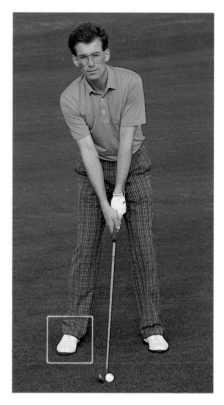

1 FEET TOGETHER
Stand with your feet fairly close together and the ball placed exactly in the middle of your stance. Carefully position the clubface square to your ball-to-target line.

2 LEFT FOOT POINTS OUT
Keeping your right foot in place, plant your left foot comfortably to one side. The left foot should point slightly outwards throughout your swing action to promote an effective and balanced body turn.

3 BALL DEAD CENTRE
Move your right foot the same distance from the ball as your left so that the ball is in the centre of your stance. Shifting one foot at a time keeps the clubface square and helps you maintain good balance from the outset.

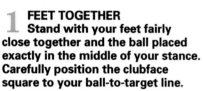

pro tip

Try the hand span test
To make sure that you're standing the correct distance away from the ball, check how far your body is from the top of the club.

After setting up as normal, take your right hand off the club. Place your little finger on your left thigh and your thumb on the butt of the club. A comfortable hand span – neither stretched nor compressed – confirms the correct distance.

When the ball is too far from your body you're likely to hit off the toe of the club, losing power and control. A hook is also probable.

With the ball too near your body the heel of the club strikes the ball, so you may shank. A slice is also a strong possibility.

you stand from the ball at address.

When you swing the longer shafted clubs, you stand more upright and slightly further away from the ball than you do with – for instance – an 8 iron. This leads to a flatter swing plane than with the shorter clubs, when you're more bent over.

SPLIT SECOND TIMING

Whatever the club, and whatever the shot, the clubface is square for only a fraction of a second during the swing. That's why ball position is so vital – it must be perfect to receive the clubhead in that split second.

Spend time practising these changes in stance width and ball position. They must become automatic so that you know you can always swing from a solid base. This skill does not emerge overnight – it may take an entire season before your set-up becomes second nature and your ball position reliable.

Curing posture problems

Before you start your swing, you must position your body properly as you address the ball. Correct posture is vital because it is the basis of an effective golf swing. Although you may feel happy with how you stand, faults can creep in easily and cause problems with your game.

Begin by making sure that you're playing with suitable clubs. Their length and lie must suit your height and arm length.

STAND POISED AND READY
Whatever your build and height you should be able to keep faults from creeping into your posture. Stand comfortably at address in almost a semi-sitting position, feeling poised and ready for action. Your back should stay reasonably straight – make sure you don't stoop.

See a qualified PGA pro to check these essentials – without them you have no chance of swinging to your potential. More importantly, you also risk back pain and injury if you strain too many of the wrong muscles.

BE COMFORTABLE

Treat your posture as a way of moving your body into a relaxed, comfortable position, so that you're poised and ready for action. When you get it right, you are perfectly balanced throughout your swing, because your arms, legs and body can move freely and without strain.

If your knees are locked your spine leans over too much, restrict-ing your muscle movement. Bending your knees a lot forces you to crouch over the ball, so that making a full shoulder turn is very hard.

YOUR STANCE

Stance is an important ingredient of the correct posture. It promotes balance and helps control. Take your stance by setting the insides of your feet the same distance apart as your shoulders.

Narrow your stance for the shorter clubs and widen it for the longer clubs and woods. Too narrow a stance makes you badly balanced and restricts upper body

SHORT

AVERAGE

TALL

HOW GOOD IS YOUR POSTURE?

movement.

Point your left foot (right foot if you strike left handed) slightly outwards – it must point in the direction that your body is turning as you strike the ball. Pointing your left foot inwards badly hampers your movement and causes physical strain.

POSTURE EXERCISE

When your stance is sound, you can prepare your posture. The point of changing your body position from its normal upright bearing is to create a sturdy yet balanced starting block for the golf swing.

To practise proper posture, think of being almost in a semi-sitting position. Hold a club lengthways across the back of your shoulders. Lean forward from your upper body only, then flex your knees, making sure that you're still comfortable for the swing.

Your upper body should be still

GOOD: KEEP MOVING
Correct posture is vital as it is the foundation of a good golf swing. Relax and keep your body moving so that you don't adopt faults. Feel live tension in your arms and legs. Keep your back fairly straight.

GOOD: AT THE TARGET
With a correct posture and a good swing, the club points directly at the target at the top of the backswing. Your lower body must stay flexed and fluid, letting your weight transfer smoothly.

OVERBENDING YOUR KNEES
Bending your knees too much makes you crouch over the ball. Your back is severely bent and you feel extremely uncomfortable.

NO SHOULDER TURN
As you've bent over so far, you lift rather than swing the club, pointing it left of target. You make very little shoulder turn, giving you no chance of a complete backswing.

reasonably upright and straight – be careful not to stoop as it gives you no chance of swinging to your potential.

Your weight should be spread evenly and your lower legs should feel lively – as if they have springs in them.

When you lower your head to look at the ground, bend your neck – not your shoulders. If your shoulders are too far forward, you're in danger of crouching, which ruins your chances of making a full turn.

ARM POSITION

Once you feel happy in the correct position, take the club from behind your shoulders and grip normally.

Your arms form a V shape, with the left arm hanging straight while the right is a little bent at the elbow – which helps keep away pre-swing stiffness and tension.

Check that your elbows are in a good position by making sure that they point at their respective hipbones. Try to let your arms and the club form one unit throughout the swing.

STAY RELAXED

Now that you're in position and ready to swing it's vital to remain calm and comfortable so you maintain good posture.

Every moving part of your body must be poised and ready for action – otherwise your swing becomes laboured and stilted.

Keep your feet, knees and shoulders lively by making little movements and waggling the club a few times.

This process tunes you up for your swing – as well as keeping you relaxed in the correct, comfortable posture you need to make a full swing.

Check the span
Make sure you are holding the club the proper distance from your body by spanning your right hand from the top of the shaft to your left thigh. If it reaches comfortably – so that you don't have to stretch or bunch your fingers – you're spot on.

LOCKED KNEES
Straight and stiff legs at address make you lean forward too much as you address the ball. Your body has no chance of fluid movement.

BAD BALANCE AND TURN
It proves impossible to rotate your hips and shoulders to their full extent. Adequate weight transfer and balance become very difficult.

Watch your feet position
Locked knees and toes pointing inwards (left) restrict leg movement. Too much tension in your lower body stops you making a positive swing. Stand with your feet the same distance apart as your shoulders and point your toes out (right) to promote strong hip turn.

pro tip

Sit on a shooting stick
Imagine you're sitting on a shooting stick. This encourages you to bend your knees from the thighs down. As your knees bend, your back should stay quite straight with your body still upright. Don't use your hips when flexing your knees.

PRACTISE YOUR POSTURE

KEEP A STRAIGHT BACK
To practise the almost semi-sitting position – and reasonably straight back – you need for perfect posture, hold a club lengthways across the back of your shoulders. Lean forward with your upper body only and then flex your knees from the thighs down.

SPREAD YOUR WEIGHT
Make sure your neck – not your shoulders – is bent over and that your weight is evenly spread. Then turn a full 90° – there will be tension in your legs. Turn back and through, so your body twists as far left as it can go.

IMPROVE BALANCE AND IMPACT

If you were to watch leading professionals hitting shots on a practice ground, you would notice a variation in their swings. You would watch in awe as they produced great shots time after time without appreciating that they all maintain perfect balance throughout the swing and achieve the same impact position. Concentrate on good balance as you would any other part of the swing.

Lee Trevino says he has a 'compensatory' swing – it contains flaws, but each one is matched by a compensating movement.

Perfecting your balance

The golf swing is an exercise that has an uncanny knack of upsetting an otherwise impeccable sense of balance. Staying firmly planted on your own two feet sounds simple enough, but it still manages to elude many club players.

The fault is so common because many golfers regard balance as an unimportant aspect of the swing – therefore they don't feel the need to work on it. They're so tied up with straight left arm, head down and coiled upper body that they forget about the movement of their feet and overall balance. It's an attitude that cannot possibly produce consistent results.

Don't make striking the ball more difficult than it already is. Be sure that you pay at least as much attention to perfecting your balance as you do to any other part of the swing.

ON AN EVEN FOOTING

There are times when keeping your balance is not easy, so you need to know how to cope. Even golfers who appear rock solid over the ball and during the swing can be prone to a slight wobble. Wild and windy days on an exposed links are often the cause of the problem – gusting breezes buffet you as you fight to stay steady.

In these testing conditions you need to work doubly hard at maintaining your balance – not just over the full shots but from close range too.

Widen your stance a fraction to give yourself a more solid foundation over the ball. Shorten your swing to make it more compact and less vulnerable to a battering from the wind – this has the added benefit of helping you hit the ball lower than normal.

If you have a long, willowy swing you're especially likely to suffer from balance problems in the wind. Bear in mind that the more compact you make your swing the better it stands up in gusty conditions. Picture Ian Woosnam's swing for example. Solid, straightforward – he's one

▶ **STUMBLING BLOCK**
The tell-tale signs of poor balance are easy to spot. All the body weight moves away from the target instead of flowing on to the left side. This technique destroys all hope of striking the ball correctly because the clubhead is on an upward path at impact. You're likely to block the ball out to the right. The cardinal rule of iron play is to strike down on the ball – impossible to achieve if your balance is so out of control that you topple backwards on the downswing.

◀ **BALANCED FINISH**
Good and bad together is an excellent combination when trying to identify specific faults. This is a fine example and highlights the benefits to be gained by keeping your balance. You can transfer your weight smoothly on to the left side which enables you to strike down and through the ball. The classic finish you achieve is an additional benefit – while it's too late to influence the path of the ball it still looks impressive.

KEEP IT COMPACT IN THE WIND

1 STABLE ADDRESS
Every golfer is exposed to strong winds, so make sure you practise the techniques and shots that are best suited to these testing conditions. The low punch shot is a precious stroke – it keeps both the ball and your score down when the wind is straight in your face. Forget the distance you usually hit your approach shots – a 7 iron can be used from the 100yd (90m) mark as long as you stay in control. Place your feet wider apart than normal with the ball central in your stance – this looks and feels like a compact address position.

2 STEADY START
From a stable position at address you're in perfect shape to make a good takeaway – essential to the overall success of the shot. Sweep the club back and concentrate on making a one piece takeaway. Resist the temptation to become very wristy – this is a trap that many club golfers fall into when playing in the wind. If you pick the club up too steeply you're likely to strike down on a similar angle of attack which generates too much backspin. The ball starts low, but climbs too quickly and falls short of the target.

3 SHORT AT THE TOP
Control is the name of the game when you play this type of shot, so stop the club well short of horizontal at the top of the backswing. This serves a dual purpose in that the shorter you swing the club the more likely your technique is to stand up well in the wind. Remember, you should be doing all you can to resist buffeting from the breeze. Try to think of this as a shortened version of the full swing – note how the shoulders have turned and the weight is mostly positioned on the right side.

4 TOP TO BOTTOM

The split second that it takes to go from the top of the backswing to impact is such that you cannot deliberately link the moves together – it all happens too fast for the brain to react. It's vital to start the downswing correctly – you then give yourself the best possible chance of arriving at a good impact position.

As you pull the butt of the club down, slide your knees towards the target to help shift your weight on to the left side. Feel your hands leaving the clubhead behind – this guarantees they're ahead of the ball at impact to promote crisp contact.

5 PUNCHED FOLLOWTHROUGH

The ball is on its way but there's still work to do. You need to punch the clubhead through low towards the target. To help you, imagine a small coin about 12in (30cm) in front of the ball along the intended line, then visualize the clubhead travelling directly over that

point. Concentrate on staying down on the shot – your knees play a vital role in achieving this by remaining comfortably flexed through impact. With most of your weight now on the left side you can complete the swing the way you started it – simple, compact and perfectly balanced.

DRIVING IN CALM CONDITIONS

1 ROCK STEADY
Even when there isn't a breath of wind you still need to concentrate hard on maintaining your balance. This is especially true when you have the driver in your hands – it's this more than any other club that causes golfers almost to throw themselves at the ball which ultimately results in a loss of balance.

2 ADDRESS TO TAKEAWAY
Sweep the club back close to the ground for at least the first 12in (30cm) of the backswing – this is one of the more popular pieces of advice because it concerns one of the most important moves in the swing. The straight line formed at address by your left arm and the shaft of the club should have altered very little at this stage of the swing.

3 SWING ACTIVATOR
This is the first clear sign of the swing starting to take shape and is a fine example of one good move leading to another. Taking the club back low to the ground sets the necessary wide arc – this in turn pulls the upper body into a coiled position and starts to shift your weight towards the right side.

4 TURNING POINT
Halfway through the swing you should feel in complete control of your balance. Whether you reach horizontal at the top of the backswing is really a matter of personal choice – a lot depends on how supple you are. Just short is a good position because it gives you time to turn fully and yet still remain in control.

5 BALANCING ACT
A smooth transfer of weight on to the left side helps you keep your balance in the hitting area. Note the good extension through the ball – clubhead speed should almost pull you into the followthrough. If ever golfers suffer from poor balance it tends to be at this stage of the swing – usually caused by a frantic lunge from the top.

6 HAPPY ENDING
This more than any other part of the swing is where you can spot the difference between good and bad balance. It's the followthrough position achieved by every professional and is something you can learn from and copy yourself. You can only finish the swing in impressive fashion like this by transferring your weight correctly and maintaining your balance.

of the finest wind players in the world.

When you have to play a shot from a viciously sloping lie, you need to counteract the imbalance by slightly altering your weight distribution.

As a rule you need to go against the slope. With the ball well below the level of your feet, shift a little more of your weight on to your heels to prevent you toppling forwards when you swing. Move your weight more towards your toes to help you cope with a ball above your feet.

BALANCE OF POWER

In calm conditions on reasonably flat ground there are no excuses for losing your balance. For the full shots you must maintain good balance because it helps you transfer your weight with control throughout the swing.

Your weight moves away from the ball on the backswing and on to the left side through impact. When you carry this out smoothly you enhance your power. But if your balance is slightly out, you upset both your rhythm and timing. This is certain to have a disastrous effect on the strike.

Perfect balance also consistently helps you keep the clubhead on the correct swing plane throughout.

When you see a golfer with poor balance, look at the direction the clubhead travels during the swing – it's unlikely to stay on the same plane from start to finish. A more likely scenario is that as the player topples from one poor position to another, the clubhead is unavoidably thrown out of plane.

Your swing plane in turn has an effect on the path of the clubhead through impact. When the plane is consistent you can more accurately control the direction of the clubhead as it meets the ball – one good move results from another earlier in the swing.

Short game stance
Windy conditions often play havoc as your ball flies through the air, but don't pretend the problems come to an end there. When you move closer to the hole there are other difficulties you need to contend with.

The key to holding your short game together in strong winds is keeping still over the ball and staying balanced. To achieve this, take every step possible to build a solid and compact stance for both your chipping and putting.

Stand with your feet slightly wider apart than normal. This establishes a good foundation and helps prevent any unwanted movement over the ball. You probably know from experience how important this can be to the shot. There's nothing more distracting than feeling a strong gust of wind just as you're about to start your takeaway.

Fall over backwards
Toppling backwards is a very common fault among handicap golfers. Sufferers are bound to be plagued by inconsistency and disappointment.

If your weight moves away from the target on the downswing you can forget about hitting the ball well – even from a good position at the top of the backswing. More often than not the shot goes horribly wrong.

The fault happens because the arc of your swing moves backwards along with you. This immediately destroys any good work you may have done earlier such as setting up to the ball correctly. As you come down there is little hope of making good contact – the clubhead either thuds into the ground before the ball, or travels up at the point of impact resulting in an ugly thinned shot.

Remember, a slight sway from the target is fine on the backswing. But you must transfer your weight on to the left side on the downswing – failure to do so can only end in poor strikes.

Impact

The impact position is the point during the swing when you're about to strike the ball. It's the moment when – if you swing correctly – the clubhead finally catches up with your hands.

To hit a golf ball both long and straight down the fairway, you must return the clubhead to the ball with two qualities – power and accuracy.

Your body position at impact differs for irons and woods, but ball position and shaft length combine to alter the strike. With woods, no divot is taken as you sweep the ball – which is opposite your left heel – off the fairway or tee peg.

To gain top benefit from an iron club, it's vital to strike the ball first, before taking a small divot. Move the ball towards the centre of your stance as the shaft length shortens.

SQUARE CLUBFACE

There are many different types of correct golf swing – but only one correct impact position. This means returning the clubface squarely to the ball, which leads to straight hitting. Building power is more complicated.

You coil power in the backswing – this power is stored at the top. As your downswing begins, your lower body starts a weight shift to the left and your shoulders, arms and hands follow, before finally releasing the clubhead at impact.

Being in the proper impact

ONE IMPACT POSITION
Although there are many types of golf swing, there is only one impact position. It's similar to the set-up – the clubface is square to the ball, but the lower body is shifting left.

INCORRECT: NO LOWER BODY MOVEMENT

CLUB STAYS AHEAD
Starting your swing with your shoulders and failing to move your lower body left means that most of your weight stays firmly fixed on the right. You swing the clubface across the line, which closes the clubface and causes a slice.

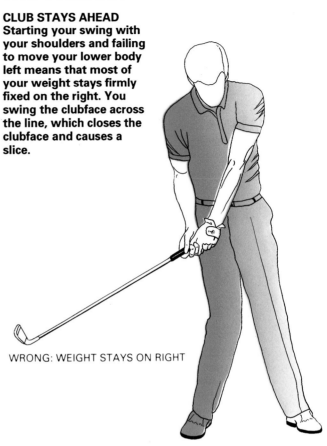

WRONG: WEIGHT STAYS ON RIGHT

INCORRECT: MOVING AHEAD

EARLY WEIGHT TRANSFER
As you start the downswing, you shift your weight too quickly to the left, and you move ahead of the clubhead. At impact the club has no chance of catching up, usually causing an open clubface – and a push.

WRONG: WEIGHT SHIFTS TOO EARLY

PRACTISE YOUR HAND POSITION

1 ADDRESS
Stand with knees flexed in your normal address position. Hold out both arms in front of you, as if about to take grip.

2 TOP OF BACKSWING
Leave your left arm straight and swing your right arm to the top of the backswing position. Slowly move your hips back to the left, keeping your knees bent.

3 IMPACT
Look at your hand positions. They should have returned to impact solely through lower body movement. No conscious hand action should be needed.

CORRECT WEIGHT SHIFT THROUGH IMPACT

CLUBHEAD CATCHES UP WITH HANDS
As you start your downswing, your left hip turns to the left – enough to transfer your weight to your left foot. This movement lowers your hands and arms to the mid point position. You should feel very powerful, with both arms loaded with energy. The muscles in your left hip

and thigh keep turning smoothly to the left and your right leg and knee follow. Your lower body is taut but springy. The shot does not finish with the strike – your weight continues to your left side, letting your upper body turn and face the target. This movement brings your head up to watch the ball's flight.

pro tip

USE AN UMBRELLA

Drive an umbrella into the ground and set up as normal with the outside of your left foot (right foot for left-handers) touching the umbrella. Make your usual swing.

You're in the correct position at impact if your left knee touches the umbrella, but the space remains between your hip and the umbrella.

position ensures that you achieve maximum distance and the correct trajectory. If you're out of position, you're likely to hit fat (behind the ball) or thin (halfway up).

HIP ACTION

To hit squarely at impact, you must start the downswing with the correct hip action by turning your hips smoothly left.

Feel as if your hips pull the arms and hands down until the mid point of the downswing, when your arms should be loaded with power. Your shoulders send power to your arms, the arms to the hands and your hands pass it on to the clubhead.

If everything else is as it should be, the clubface is square on contact. Don't try to control the clubface at this point – it's moving far too quickly.

At impact, the clubhead, arms and hands form a straight line, although your position is not identical to the one you adopt at set-up. This is because your lower body carries on turning to the left, so that your weight shifts fully from your right side. Keep your head steady.

Remember that you haven't finished playing the shot when you strike the ball – it's important to make a full follow through.

3

SHOTS THAT RUIN YOUR SCORES

Always unpredictable, golf can also be frustrating because you never know what sort of shot you are going to hit. With the possibility of slicing, hooking, topping or even thinning, all on the same hole, it is important to understand what causes poor shots. The one thing that separates the low handicappers from the high is that the former are more aware of the do's and don'ts.

If a shot lands in dense woodland, it saves time to play a provisional ball before you search for the lost original. Declare your ball as provisional or it becomes the ball in play.

Curing the slice 1

INCORRECT ADDRESS
A slice may arise from several different errors. It can be a fault in your grip, body alignment, ball position and angle of clubface.

You slice if you grip the club too tightly or wrongly, align your body left or right of the target, place the ball too far forward in your stance or open the clubface at address.

At address you must have a relaxed grip, be aligned parallel to the ball-to-target line and aim the clubface squarely.

CORRECT ADDRESS

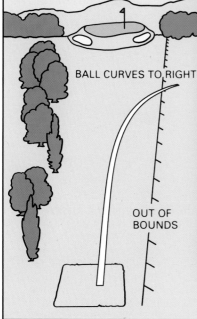

The destructive slice
A slice is an uncontrolled shot that curves to the right. It is very destructive, especially if there are hazards or out of bounds on that same side. You lose distance, direction and strokes so it's important to correct this common fault.

BALL CURVES TO RIGHT

OUT OF BOUNDS

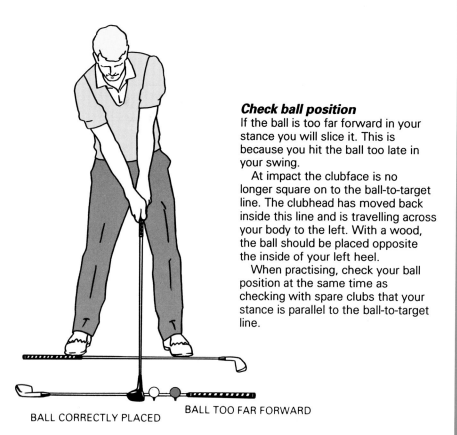

BALL CORRECTLY PLACED

BALL TOO FAR FORWARD

Check ball position

If the ball is too far forward in your stance you will slice it. This is because you hit the ball too late in your swing.

At impact the clubface is no longer square on to the ball-to-target line. The clubhead has moved back inside this line and is travelling across your body to the left. With a wood, the ball should be placed opposite the inside of your left heel.

When practising, check your ball position at the same time as checking with spare clubs that your stance is parallel to the ball-to-target line.

ALIGNMENT PROBLEM

SHOULDERS POINT LEFT OF TARGET

STANCE ALIGNED LEFT OF TARGET

BALL-TO-TARGET LI

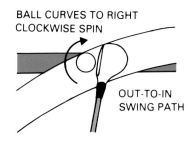

BALL CURVES TO RIGHT CLOCKWISE SPIN

OUT-TO-IN SWING PATH

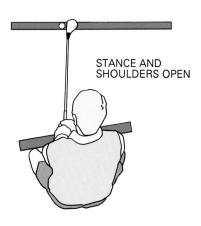

STANCE AND SHOULDERS OPEN

Body aligned left (incorrect)

If your body is aligned left of the target you take the clubhead away outside the ball-to-target line. From here it is difficult to return it squarely and the downswing usually follows the same path as the backswing.

The slice is the most common fault in golf. It is an uncontrolled shot in which the ball curves to the right of the ball-to-target line, causing you to lose direction and distance.

Most slices are the result of an unintentional out-to-in swing path, though other faults may also produce slicing. Whatever the swing path, the clubface always moves across the ball from far right to near left. This causes the ball to spin in a clockwise direction, which moves the ball from left to right as it flies through the air.

Faults that lead to a slice occur at either the address position or during the swing itself. This chapter deals with errors at address which can be caused by a bad grip, an open clubface, wrong body alignment or an incorrect ball position.

GRIP PRESSURE

A slice can result from gripping the club too tightly. This creates tension in your upper body, which restricts movement and prevents you from turning correctly. Your upper body, arms and hands pull the clubhead around your body and across the ball from right to left – on an out-to-in swing path.

It is vital to check grip pressure regularly. When you grip a club, imagine you're holding a bird in your hand. If you hold it too loosely it can flap its wings or even escape, while gripping it too tightly squashes it. Ideally, the bird should not be able to move but must not be harmed either.

The correct grip pressure allows your hands, wrists, arms and upper body to swing freely. Your hands, wrists and arms must feel relaxed at address and during the swing.

OPEN CLUBFACE

A tight grip can also lead to an open clubface at impact. If you hold the club too tightly your hands don't turn naturally through the ball and the clubface doesn't return to its position at address. The clubface stays slightly open and the ball flies to the right.

Unintentionally opening the clubface at address is the most obvious fault in an otherwise good stroke.

The clubhead still travels through

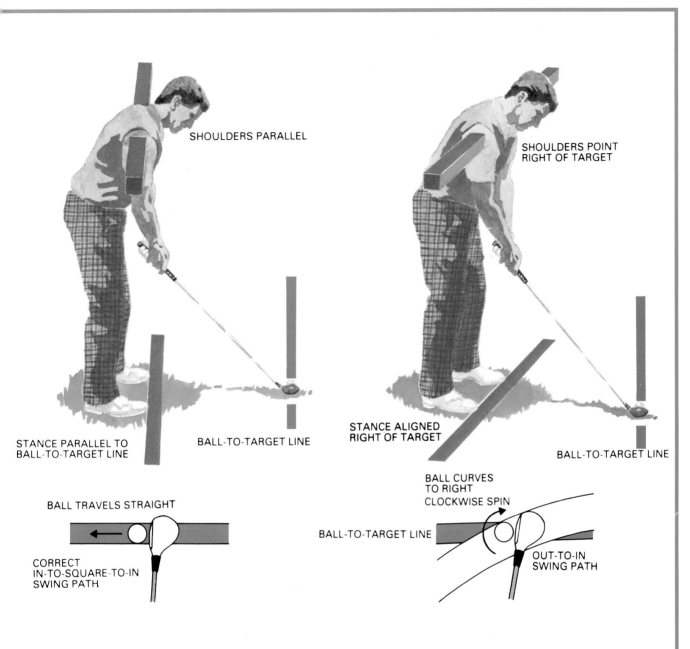

SHOULDERS PARALLEL

SHOULDERS POINT RIGHT OF TARGET

STANCE PARALLEL TO BALL-TO-TARGET LINE

BALL-TO-TARGET LINE

STANCE ALIGNED RIGHT OF TARGET

BALL-TO-TARGET LINE

BALL TRAVELS STRAIGHT

CORRECT IN-TO-SQUARE-TO-IN SWING PATH

BALL CURVES TO RIGHT CLOCKWISE SPIN

BALL-TO-TARGET LINE

OUT-TO-IN SWING PATH

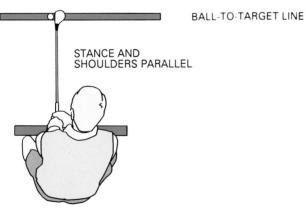

BALL-TO-TARGET LINE

STANCE AND SHOULDERS PARALLEL

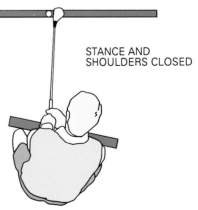

STANCE AND SHOULDERS CLOSED

Body aligned parallel (correct)
Align your body parallel to the ball-to-target line. This makes it easier to take the clubhead away correctly on the backswing and return the clubface squarely on the downswing.

Body aligned right (incorrect)
When your body points to the right of the target, you still try to swing through impact on the ball-to-target line. You pull the club across your body and this can produce an out-to-in swing path and a slice.

Check your grip
As well as too tight a grip, a weak – wrongly placed – grip can cause a slice.

You have a weak (slicer's) grip if you can see only one or less than one knuckle on your left hand and you can't see the 'V' between the thumb and forefinger on your right hand. With this type of grip it is difficult to control the clubhead because your hands don't turn easily through impact. The clubface stays open and you slice the ball.

With a correct grip you see two to three knuckles of your left hand, and the 'V' on your right hand points between your chin and right shoulder.

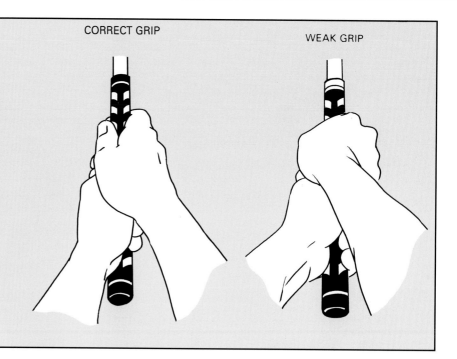

CORRECT GRIP

WEAK GRIP

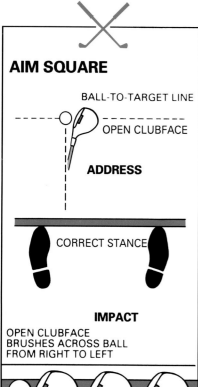

AIM SQUARE

BALL-TO-TARGET LINE

OPEN CLUBFACE

ADDRESS

CORRECT STANCE

IMPACT

OPEN CLUBFACE BRUSHES ACROSS BALL FROM RIGHT TO LEFT

CORRECT IN-TO-SQUARE-TO-IN SWING PATH

An open clubface at address ends in a slice – even if the rest of your set-up and swing is perfect. Although the clubhead follows the correct in-to-square-to-in swing path, an open clubface at impact brushes across the back of the ball. This imparts sidespin and the ball goes right.

impact on the correct in-to-square-to-in swing path but the clubface doesn't meet the ball square on. It brushes across the back of the ball causing it to start right of the ball-to-target line and then spin further to the right.

Always check that the clubface is aimed correctly. A slightly open clubface can ruin a good set-up and swing.

BODY ALIGNMENT

Misalignment also causes you to slice. At address your shoulders, chest, hips and feet should be aligned parallel to the ball-to-target line.

If your stance, hips, chest and shoulders point right of the ball-to-target line, you try to compensate by swinging the clubhead towards the target. This drags your right shoulder across the ball from right to left (out to in).

If you align left of the target it is impossible for your upper body to rotate correctly. You take the clubhead away outside the ball-to-target line on the backswing and the downswing follows the same path. The result is an out-to-in swing through impact, which leaves you struggling to recover from a slice.

INCORRECT BALL POSITION

Always check your ball position carefully. Even if your grip, alignment and swing path are correct,

you can still slice if the ball is placed too far forward in your stance. Impact is delayed and the club-face is no longer square on to the ball-to-target line. The clubhead has moved back inside this line and is travelling to the left. The clubface brushes across the ball from right to left, imparting un-wanted sidespin.

Remember that correct ball position differs from club to club. For a wood and a long iron place the ball opposite the inside of your left heel. For a short iron the ball is in the centre of your stance, while for a medium iron you need to place the ball midway between the two positions.

pro tip

Limit your slice
It is risky to try to correct a slice during a round. If you find you are slicing most of your tee shots, compensate for the fault rather than fight it. Instead of looking for an immediate cure, limit its effect for the rest of your round.

Stop driving with a 1 or 2 wood, and move down to a number 3 which won't hit the ball as far – so the distance the ball travels off-line is reduced. The extra loft and shorter shaft of the 3 wood also give more control. When you tee off, aim a little further left than normal.

When the round is complete, analyse your technique to eliminate the slice.

Curing the slice 2

Problems at address may lead to an incorrect swing path and a slice, but you can produce the same poor shot from a faulty swing alone.

Errors that create an unwanted out-to-in swing path can occur on the backswing and throughswing. These faults lead to the clubface brushing across the ball from left to right, giving a slice.

BODY ROTATION

The most common cause of the slice is lack of body rotation, a flowing movement which shapes the swing. The individual parts of your body must move as one unit.

If your body fails to turn correctly and fully, your arms and hands shape the swing. Working on their own, these take the club away outside the ball-to-target line. From this position it's difficult to return the clubhead on the correct in-to-square-to-in swing path.

The downswing usually follows the same path as the backswing, so the clubhead is pulled incorrectly across your body from far right to near left (out to in).

Although the effect is always the same, lack of rotation has many

SWING SLICE
A slice is usually the result of a poor swing which produces an untidy and unbalanced finish. Your weight transfers incorrectly and your body finishes up facing the wrong direction. The result – a slice.

POOR HEAD MOVEMENT
If your head fails to move together with your rotating body you can't turn freely.

LACK OF SHOULDER ROTATION
You can't shape your swing correctly if your shoulders don't turn enough.

UPPER BODY TENSION
Faults in your swing can be exaggerated by errors at address. If your grip is too tight, your upper body becomes tense and fails to rotate fully.

POOR WEIGHT TRANSFER
If your body rotates incorrectly, you finish the swing with your weight on the wrong foot.

PREVENTING A SLICE

CORRECT – CLUBHEAD INSIDE BALL-TO-TARGET LINE

CORRECT – CLUBHEAD POINTS AT TARGET

1 TAKEAWAY FAULTS
The start of the backswing establishes the swing path. To avoid an out-to-in path on the downswing, don't take the clubhead outside the ball-to-target line. Let the clubhead move gradually inside this line on takeaway.

2 TOP OF THE BACKSWING
Unless your body has rotated fully on the backswing there isn't any power to unleash on the downswing. If you lift the club outside the ball-to-target line, the shaft doesn't point to the target at the top of the backswing.

CORRECT FOLLOWTHROUGH – FACING TARGET

5 UNBALANCED FOLLOWTHROUGH
An out-to-in swing path pulls the club across your body on the followthrough and your weight finishes up awkwardly on the tip of your right foot. Always try to achieve a balanced finish with your weight on the left foot and your body facing the target.

pro tip

Keep your chin up
For your shoulders and chest to rotate properly there must be a clear gap between the tip of your chin and the top of your shoulders. If your chin drops too low it gets in the way of your upper body and prevents it from turning fully.

CORRECT DOWNSWING AND WEIGHT TRANSFER

CORRECT – GOOD IMPACT AND THROUGHSWING

3 TRANSFER OF WEIGHT
If your weight is not on your right foot at the top of the backswing your hands and arms can't follow the correct swing path on the downswing – they usually swing independently across your body. Just over half your weight should transfer on to your left foot by impact.

4 ROTATION THROUGH IMPACT
If upper body movement is restricted through impact, the momentum of your hands and arms pulls the clubhead across the ball from right to left. Your upper body must continue to rotate to the left to pull the clubhead through the ball on the correct in-to-square-to-in path.

causes. Failing to turn the body on the backswing is a common problem for players who believe that the less body movement you have, the more compact and efficient your swing is.

While a swing needs to be compact, it must also be shaped by the rotation of your body as a unit and not as a mixture of different moving parts – such as your arms and hands. These must remain passive until impact.

HEAD MOVEMENT

Lack of rotation is also caused by poor head movement. Many golfers who obediently keep their eye on the ball follow this rule to the extreme by not moving their heads at all. If your head does not rotate with your upper body, overall movement is restricted.

Even if head movement is correct on the backswing, problems can creep in if your head stays down too long on the throughswing.

The moment that your head stops turning freely it prevents your right shoulder from rotating towards the target, and your arms and hands pull the clubhead across

One bad turn leads to another
One fault leads to another so it is vital that you practise your backswing until it is correct in every detail.

If your body doesn't rotate fully, you lift the club outside the ball-to-target line and at the top of the backswing your weight has not transferred on to your right foot.

From this point it is difficult to return the clubhead squarely, and you swing it across your body. You are left with an unbalanced finish.

POOR SHOULDER TURN

UNBALANCED FOLLOWTHROUGH

your body to the left. You complete the followthrough awkwardly, with your weight on the wrong foot and the clubhead pointing to the left.

THE HALF SWING

Develop correct body rotation and head movement by practising the half swing. This makes it easier to judge how your body is moving, and to gauge the passage of the clubhead. You are also more relaxed than during a full swing.

Concentrate on letting your shoulders rotate freely through impact so your body faces the target at completion of the swing.

This automatically brings your head up to face the same direction. Allow your upper body to rotate as one. By rotating on the downswing and followthrough, your arms and hands swing smoothly through the ball.

Shape body rotation
To develop the correct body rotation on the throughswing, follow this simple practice routine. Take a club in your left hand and hold your left wrist in your right hand. Then make a normal swing keeping your right elbow tucked into your side.

As you swing through impact your right arm prevents your right side from swinging across the ball. This shapes the swing correctly – the clubhead moves inside the ball-to-target line.

Checklist
If you keep slicing the ball, run through this checklist to see where the problem is – it can be caused at address or during the swing. It's important to cure any bad habits before they become ingrained.

Grip pressure: are you gripping the club too tightly?

Ball position: are you teeing the ball too far forward in your stance?

Alignment: is your body incorrectly aligned left or right of the target?

Clubface: is an open clubface at address causing you to slice?

Grip position: can you see two to three knuckles on your left hand, with the 'V' between the thumb and forefinger of your right hand pointing between your right shoulder and chin? If not you are gripping incorrectly.

Body rotation: are you failing to rotate your body enough?

Head movement: are you keeping your head down too long?

Umbrella tip
You can eliminate a swing problem by placing an umbrella against the tip of your left foot. This stops you swinging across your body – from out to in – because your hands hit the umbrella if you do. Practise frequently and you should eliminate the out-to-in swing path.

Throwing your right shoulder

UPPER BODY STOPS ROTATING

RIGHT SHOULDER, ARMS AND HANDS PULL CLUBHEAD ACROSS BALL-TO-TARGET LINE

BALL CURVES TO RIGHT

CORRECT PARALLEL STANCE

One of the main causes of the slice is the failure of your hands, arms, shoulders, chest and hips to work as a unit. Even if your stance and ball position are correct, this prevents the swing from being shaped properly.

If your upper body doesn't turn fully on the backswing, you tend to throw your right shoulder across the ball-to-target line on the downswing.

Curing topped shots

Topping the ball is a common fault – especially among beginners and high handicappers. The error happens when you strike the ball close to the top, applying topspin so that it pops up and down along the ground.

Every golfer fears the topped shot – as well as adding to your score it looks embarrassing. But once you know why you top, you can rid your game of it for good.

Your purpose with the longer shafted clubs is to make the club strike through the back of the ball. With the shorter clubs, when you

WHAT TOPPING IS
When you strike at or near the top of the ball it scuttles along the surface or is pressed into the ground before jumping into the air a short distance. Fix your mind on making contact with the back of the ball to avoid a topped shot.

CLUB SOLE STRIKES
TOP OF BALL -
APPLIES DAMAGING TOPSPIN

WATCH YOUR WEIGHT SHIFT

1 TOP OF BACKSWING
Your position at the top of the backswing is good, with the weight nicely shifted to the right. The shoulders have coiled to a full turn and your head remains still and in a good position over the ball. You have avoided three possible causes of the topped shot – your ball position is correct for the club, your grip is firm but not tight and your backswing is smooth and controlled.

2 POOR WEIGHT SHIFT
As you start the downswing, your head and body move too quickly, shifting too far to the left. Your hands and arms are left behind as your head moves forward – your weight fails to transfer smoothly. The downswing is no longer under control, the power generated on the backswing has been lost and your timing is poor.

let clubface loft lift the ball for you, the club must strike through the back before travelling underneath the ball.

This means striking down and through the ball. After making contact with the back of the ball, the club travels smoothly down under the bottom of the ball. Taking a large divot – shaped like a bank note – usually proves that you've achieved just that.

Make sure that the club doesn't dig down too much, making the divot too large – this could lead to a loss of distance.

WHY YOU TOP

● **Poor ball position** is the most obvious cause of topping, so place your ball carefully. If it is too far forward in your stance for the club you're using, you hit on the upswing. You make contact halfway up the ball – causing a thinned shot – or, worse, you top it.
● **Tension** is another cause of topping, mainly by inexperienced players who are nervous on the

pro tip

Grip tip

Make sure that you hold the club firmly but lightly. If your knuckles are white, you're gripping the club too tightly. This leads to a loss of timing in your swing because you restrict muscle movement in your arms and shoulders. The clubhead is likely to arrive at the ball at the wrong moment, possibly leading to a topped shot.

3 TOO LATE
The club arrives too late and crashes into the top of the ball at impact – this is because your hands and arms were behind your lower body movement, resulting in poor co-ordination. On this shot the weight has shifted too much to the left but take care you don't over correct the fault – leaving too much weight on the right side also leads to a topped or thinned shot.

4 LACK OF BALANCE
You finish overbalancing to the left. The ball may jump into the air before trickling only a short distance. After the shot, look for the tell-tale indentation in the ground where the ball has pressed into it. If you find that poor weight shift often leads to topped shots when you strike, practise smooth weight transfer with a mid iron and move gradually up to the woods.

Careful when you chip

When facing a gentle chip don't make the mistake of topping or thinning the ball so that it races through the back of the green.

In trying to give the ball a delicate nudge it's tempting to lift up your head and upper body with the stroke because you're keen to see the result. At the same time you lift the clubhead, giving the face no chance of striking down through the bottom of the ball. Don't quit on the stroke.

USE THE CLUBFACE LOFT

When you want the shot to gain height straight away, let the loft of the clubface do it for you – that's what it's designed for. Don't try to lift or scoop the ball (above) as you swing through. Your weight stays incorrectly on the right side throughout and the clubface has begun its upward path when it makes contact with the ball, causing a topped shot. Concentrate on taking a divot and letting your weight transfer naturally – one of golf's oddities is that you must strike *down* to get the ball *up*.

1st tee – especially if there are plenty of onlookers. Learn to blot out everything except the stroke in hand.

● **A tight grip** makes the muscles in your arms and shoulders lock, severely reducing your chances of a free-flowing swing. Relax as you address the ball and concentrate on sweeping the tee peg away as you swing through.

● **Poor weight transfer** – either too much or too little – is often the main culprit when you top. Scooping the ball with the club leaves your weight on the right side as you swing through. You're almost certain to top the ball – or catch it thin – because you strike on the upswing. How far up the ball the clubface hits determines if you top or thin the shot.

● **Chopping** at the ball results when your weight shifts left too quickly on the downswing. If you don't strike fat you top the ball down the fairway.

pro tip

Balancing act

If you're not making a clean strike on the ball, check your head movement – your head may be shifting as you swing because of body sway. Cure the fault by standing with your feet close together and hitting balls with a half swing. Concentrate on the back of the ball as you swing through. If your head moves too much you are likely to lose balance – whichever club you use.

Curing the sky

A skyed shot sends the ball almost straight up in the air and is usually hit with a driver. Though you lose distance by hitting a sky, it's one of the few bad shots that travels in the proper direction.

You aren't alone if you sky the ball. Golfers of all abilities are likely to experience the frustration of this poor shot at some time or other.

If you hit a sky don't jump to the conclusion that you are teeing the ball too high. It may be the cause from time to time, but if you often hit a sky it's unlikely to be the main reason – so teeing the

KNOWING WHY YOU SKY
Understand the reasons why you sky and you can set about trying to eliminate the shot from your game. The large divot taken by this player indicates too steep a downswing – the ball shoots uselessly high.

SKYING THE BALL

1 GOOD BACKSWING
At the top of the backswing the position is sound, with a full shoulder turn and the weight nicely transferred on to the right side. The feeling to foster at this stage is of a coiled spring about to release.

2 HIPS AHEAD
Things start to go wrong as you begin the downswing. The hips spin to the left of the target line too early, causing the club to attack the ball at too steep an angle from outside the line.

Don't slouch
Don't hunch yourself up over the ball at address. This restricts the movement in your shoulder and upper body muscles, preventing you from making a wide backswing and full shoulder turn – faults that often lead to a sky.

Dipping left shoulder
A reverse pivot – where you sway towards the ball on the backswing and dip your left shoulder – leaves you in an unbalanced position. Always transfer your weight away from the ball on the backswing.

ball lower won't solve the problem. You need to look for a fault somewhere in your swing.

A sky happens when too much of the clubface is below the centre of the ball at impact. Though it may result from poor ball positioning, it's usually caused by too steep an angle of descent on the downswing.

The ball should be swept off the tee with the driver. Never feel as though you are chopping down at the ball.

WIDE BACKSWING

Picking the club up too quickly outside the intended line on the backswing is the major cause of a sky. By taking the club back in this way, you are likely to bring the club down steeply towards the ball.

On every shot – but particularly the drive – draw the club back low and inside the line, brushing the turf with the clubhead for 12in (30cm). This helps you transfer your weight correctly on

3 WEAK LEFT SIDE
Close to impact your whole left side collapses. The hips have cleared out of the way too early and provide no support in the hitting area. The clubhead is chopping down at the ball.

4 POOR CONTACT
The position just after impact is typical of the skyed tee shot. The clubhead comes down too steeply and digs into the ground, taking a large divot. The ball travels a short distance and straight up in the air.

5 STUNTED FOLLOWTHROUGH
You are left struggling to maintain poise. The followthrough is cut short and there is no extension of the arms through the ball.

6 OFF BALANCE
A combination of earlier mistakes in the swing results in a terrible followthrough position. There is a total lack of balance as the skyed ball falls short of the target.

CHOPPING ACTION

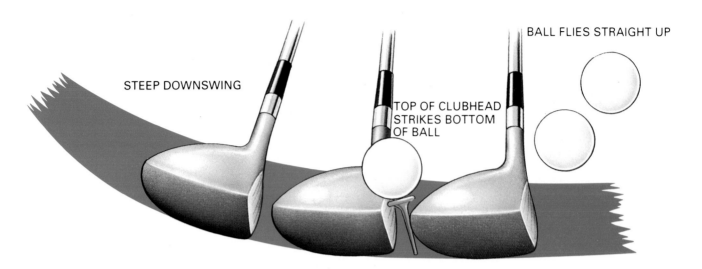

STEEP DOWNSWING

TOP OF CLUBHEAD
STRIKES BOTTOM
OF BALL

BALL FLIES STRAIGHT UP

✗ A steep angle of descent on the downswing often leads to a skyed shot. The clubhead hits below the centre of the ball, sending it upwards almost as far as it travels forwards.

With a wood, sweep the ball off the tee, letting the club loft determine the height of the shot. The head should travel parallel to the ground just before and after impact.

to the right side and make a full shoulder turn.

Don't try to hit the ball too hard. The only way to apply power on all your shots is by swinging smoothly with a gradual transfer of your weight on to your left leg on the downswing. Keep a steady tempo as you swing through – this stops you from chopping down at the ball.

USE THE LOFT

It's tempting to try and help the ball into the air by scooping in the impact area – this is a common fault with the straighter faced clubs. But the loft of the club is specifically designed to get the ball airborne – so you must trust the club to do just that. Imagine the clubhead travelling parallel to the turf about 12in (30cm) before and after making contact with the ball.

Check the ball is positioned correctly in your stance. Place it opposite your left heel at address with the driver. This encourages you to sweep the ball smoothly off the tee.

This rule applies to the wooden clubs only. An iron shot is hit best when the clubhead strikes the ball with a descending blow. So place the ball further back in your stance when you play a shot with an iron club.

pro tip

Protect your driver
Frequent skying of the ball is likely to damage your clubhead as well as ruin a good score.

When you hit a sky you fail to strike the ball with the centre of the clubface, which is designed to withstand tough treatment. Instead, the ball makes contact

with the top of the clubhead, causing ugly scuff marks.

To prevent damage to your driver, stick electrical tape carefully on the surface just above the clubface. Then work on finding a solution to stop you skying the ball.

Curing the thin shot

When the leading edge of the clubhead strikes the middle of the ball, you hit a thin (also called a sculled shot). The ball flies very low, sometimes skimming the ground, and runs a long way.

You can often get away with hitting a thinned shot. In dry conditions the ball can travel as far as a good shot – if not further – and may finish close to the intended target. It's one of those shots in golf known as a good bad one.

THIN EFFECTS

Providing the ground ahead is flat the thinned shot is often no great disaster. But put a hazard in front of you and a thin is a potential card wrecker. You can be frightened into hitting the shot you want to avoid most.

A thin can happen to you at any stage in a round of golf – from the longest iron shot down to the shortest chip.

Thinning a long iron can be upsetting, but if you hit this shot in cold weather you can add pain to your troubles. The impact of clubhead on ball vibrates up the shaft and has a numbing effect on your fingers. Massage your fin-

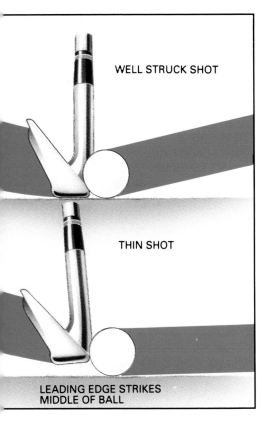

WELL STRUCK SHOT

THIN SHOT

LEADING EDGE STRIKES
MIDDLE OF BALL

▲ **AVOID THE THIN**
When faced with a shot over a hazard the tendency is to hit the ball too hard. Anxiety leads you to swing more quickly than normal – this is a frequent cause of the thinned shot. Always play within yourself. You increase your control over the clubhead and reduce the risk of hitting the thin.

REGAIN LOST TEMPO

1 RELAX AND GRIP LIGHTLY
If you're regularly thinning the ball practise some three-quarter shots with a 7 iron to help regain lost rhythm. Stand relaxed in your normal address position and grip the club lightly.

2 SMOOTH BACKSWING
Draw the club back on as wide an arc as possible – keep your movements smooth and unhurried. Never snatch the club away quickly as this throws your swing out of plane. Make a full shoulder turn.

gers as much as possible to get the feeling back into them before you hit your next shot. It's important to give yourself every chance of striking cleanly.

Always use a tee peg for your first shot on a par 3 – you give yourself a good lie and stand a better chance of making a reasonable strike on the ball. When you don't use a tee peg it's very easy to hit the ball heavy. Once you start thinking of a heavy shot, there's every chance you'll over compensate and end up thinning the ball.

SHORT SHOTS

In general the closer you are to the flag the more destructive a thin becomes. Few experiences in golf are more frustrating than watching your ball scuttle through the green and into a bunker the other side. It's easy to see how high scores can build up if you thin a lot of short shots in a round.

Number one priority is to eliminate the thinned chip from your game. Place the ball back in your stance at address and take care to

keep your hands ahead of the ball throughout the swing.

Strike down crisply and confidently – at impact it's important to concentrate on making contact with the ball first and then the turf. In golf, you must strike down to make the ball rise into the air.

If you're not comfortable with your wedge, play chip and run shots with a 7 iron to help build up your confidence. Make sure you never slow down into the ball – this is one of the major causes of the thinned shot.

Lucky escape
Never berate yourself when things go badly during a round. Take a mental note of your error; if you can't put the fault right there and then, resolve to work on it later on the practice ground.

You sometimes find you can capitalize on hitting a thin – over flat ground devoid of hazards it may finish close to the flag, while a well struck shot could bounce through the green into trouble. Accept this good fortune as a bonus rather than pondering over your poor shot – but go on working on ridding your game of the thin. Don't push your luck by relying on happy accidents.

---

pro tip

A thin cut
Look closely at your ball after you've hit a thin – it may be damaged. The leading edge of the clubhead tends to cut into the cover of a less durable golf ball. You are allowed to change it but show the ball to your playing partner first – he must agree that it is unusable.

3 THREE-QUARTER STROKE
Stop the club short of horizontal on the backswing
– by this time most of your weight should be on your
right side. This is a very controlled position from which
to strike the ball precisely.

4 WEIGHT SHIFT
Start the downswing with a gradual transfer of
weight on to your left side. Resist any temptation to
strike the ball too hard – imagine you're hitting a 7 iron
the distance of a 9 iron.

5 SMOOTH STRIKE
Stay down through impact. Your left side should
be firm to provide support in the hitting area. There's
no flurry of movement or frantic swiping at the ball –
the strike is almost effortless.

6 PERFECT RESULT
Maintaining control throughout the swing
produces a beautifully relaxed followthrough position.
It's a good test of balance if you can stand on your left
leg after completing the swing.

SLOPING LIES

The natural slope of the ground on a hanging, downhill lie (ball below feet) makes it very easy to hit a thinned shot.

The ball should be further back in your stance to compensate. This automatically reduces the loft of the club, making the ball fly lower – so remember to take one less club.

Faced with a hanging lie, flex your knees a little more than usual and bend from the waist. It's vital that you keep your head at the same level throughout the swing. If you lift your head your body will follow – and a thinned shot usually results.

Aim slightly left of target because the ball tends to fly right from a hanging lie.

GOOD SHOT

BALL RUNS THROUGH BACK OF GREEN

THIN SHOT

HANGING LIE BALL BELOW FEET

WHY DO YOU THIN?

This is an excellent position at the top of the backswing. Well balanced and poised to swing down into the back of the ball, you have total control. There's nothing hurried about this swing.

Different swing – different story. This action is known as the reverse pivot. Two faults here are typical of the thin – no transfer of weight on to the right side and a sway towards the ball on the backswing. The club is also past horizontal.

The reverse pivot makes you topple back on to your right side on the downswing – it all looks ungainly. The clubhead strikes the ball on an upward path – the club's leading edge strikes mid ball causing a thin.

SWING PATH AND SWING PLANE

There are nine ways in which to strike the ball, of which only three are acceptable. Off-line shots are due to incorrect swing path and an open or closed clubface at impact. It is important not to confuse swing path with swing plane. There is no right or wrong swing plane, which varies from person to person, but you must develop consistency as well as a style that works for you.

A good natural rhythm, plus patience and calm determination are qualities that mark out Australian Roger Davis. Here he tees off during the 1986 PGA Championship.

The nine strikes

Finding out the cause of a fault in your swing is much easier if you develop an understanding of how the clubface strikes the ball.

If you spray the ball to all points of the compass, don't simply curse your luck and move on. Ask yourself why your shots fly off target.

You can strike a golf ball in nine different ways – some desirable, others disastrous. Whatever you intend with your shot, one of those nine is sure to dictate its flight path.

When you can assess precisely which one of the nine is responsible for each shot, you find the root of any swing problem more quickly.

The two vital factors in deciding the ball's fate after impact are your swing path and the clubface posi-

tion at impact – assuming that you strike with the centre of the clubface.

The immediate direction of the ball is caused by the swing path of the club. Its direction for the rest of the shot is determined by the angle of the clubface at impact – open, closed or square – in relation to the ball-to-target line.

HIT STRAIGHT FIRST

The greatest golfers play with different styles, but they all agree on one point: the hardest shot in golf is the straight one.

For this reason, some draw the ball, others prefer to fade – but very few set out to play straight. To rely on consistent straight hitting is risky.

Straight hitting is hard because golf balls are designed to take up spin – it helps them to rise, to stop and to roll. Sidespin is also easy to apply. If you apply the correct amount of sidespin – by changing your alignment – you fade and draw the ball. Too much sidespin causes a slice or a hook.

Set your mind on hitting the ball straight before you start working on draws and fades. Concentrate on achieving an in-to-in path with a square clubface at impact by setting up parallel to the ball-to-target line.

There's a small margin of difference between a deliberate fade and a damaging slice. Only when you know how to take sidespin off the ball can you add it intentionally.

NINE POSSIBLE PATHS

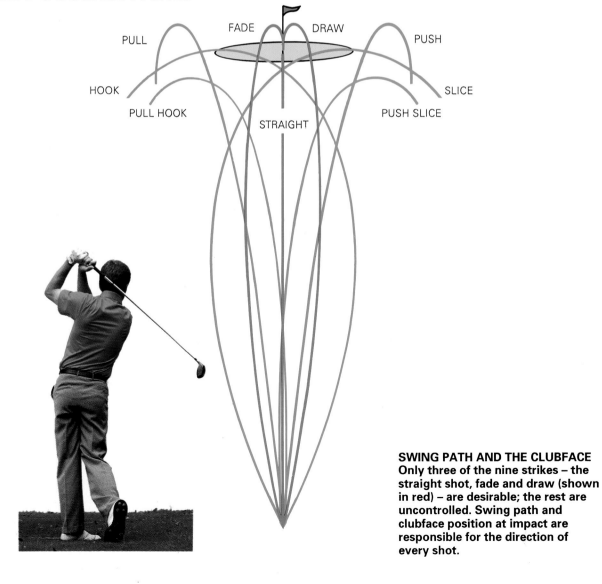

SWING PATH AND THE CLUBFACE
Only three of the nine strikes – the straight shot, fade and draw (shown in red) – are desirable; the rest are uncontrolled. Swing path and clubface position at impact are responsible for the direction of every shot.

IN-TO-OUT SWING PATH

OUT TO IN

PATH OF BALL

BALL-TO-TARGET LINE

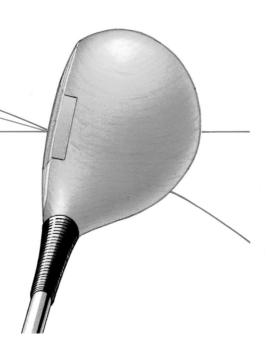

OPEN CLUBFACE

✗ **PUSH**
The club travels from inside the ball-to-target line to outside, and the clubface is open at impact. The ball travels immediately right of target in a straight line.

✗ **SLICE**
The clubhead comes from outside to inside the line, with an open clubface at impact. The ball starts left of target before curving sharply to the right.

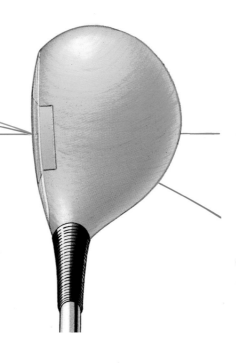

SQUARE CLUBFACE

✓ **DRAW**
Widely regarded as the ideal golf shot – because it combines distance and accuracy – the draw flies slightly right before returning to centre. It happens when the clubface meets the ball square to the ball-to-target line on an in-to-out path.

✓ **FADE**
The fade starts left of target and returns to centre, stopping quickly. The clubface is square at impact, travelling on an out-to-in path.

✗ **HOOK**
The ball starts straight – or slightly right – and curves violently left, because the clubhead has passed along an in-to-out path with the clubface closed at impact.

✗ **PULL**
The out-to-in swing path combines with the closed clubface to send the ball immediately left of target in a straight line.

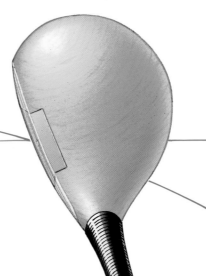
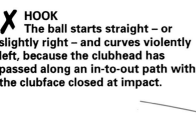

CLOSED CLUBFACE

IN TO IN

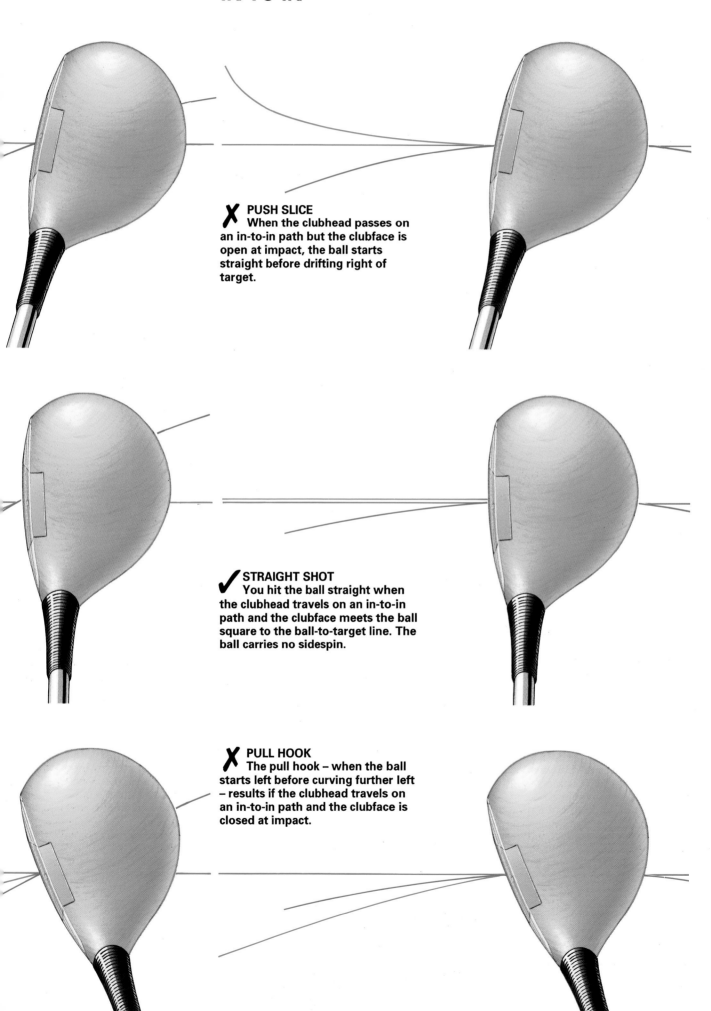

✗ PUSH SLICE
When the clubhead passes on an in-to-in path but the clubface is open at impact, the ball starts straight before drifting right of target.

✓ STRAIGHT SHOT
You hit the ball straight when the clubhead travels on an in-to-in path and the clubface meets the ball square to the ball-to-target line. The ball carries no sidespin.

✗ PULL HOOK
The pull hook – when the ball starts left before curving further left – results if the clubhead travels on an in-to-in path and the clubface is closed at impact.

pro tip

Out to in for sand play

Although you should normally try to achieve an in-to-in swing path with your straight tee, fairway and green shots, accurate greenside bunker play requires an out-to-in swing path.

The ball must normally gain height and stop quickly. Square the blade to the ball-to-target line and open your stance – this provides the extra loft you need. Your stance creates an out-to-in swing path, and the clubface is square at impact.

Keep it square when putting

If you ever struggle for accuracy on the green, always remember to return to the basics – the swing path and position of the clubface should be consistent when you're putting.

All putts are straight – the clubhead should always travel straight along the line of your putt. The clubface must be square to that line at impact, and on shorter putts should be square to it throughout the stroke.

Because of the extra backswing and throughswing needed for long putts, the path of your pendulum swing can be slightly in to in.

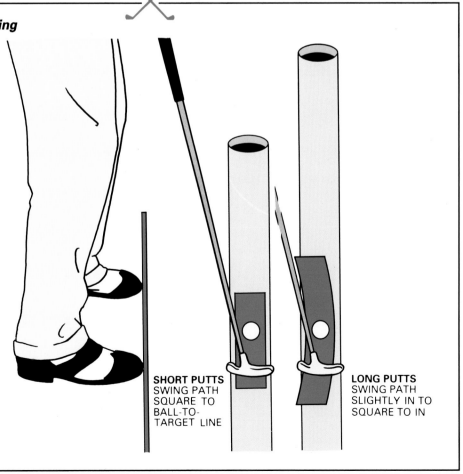

SHORT PUTTS
SWING PATH SQUARE TO BALL-TO-TARGET LINE

LONG PUTTS
SWING PATH SLIGHTLY IN TO SQUARE TO IN

Understanding swing plane

PLANE BEGINNINGS
The first part of the takeaway is crucial for setting the club on the correct swing plane. When the shaft is horizontal to the ground it should be parallel to the ball-to-target line with the clubhead pointing straight

up in the air. If you watch a professional tournament, you see many players studying this move during practice swings – notably Nick Faldo. They appreciate that it's easier to make a good swing if the first movement away from the ball

is technically sound. This is a straightforward checkpoint on a very important part of the swing. It's also an exercise you can work on by yourself on the practice ground and hence groove into your game.

HANDED ON A PLATE

1 NORMAL ADDRESS
If your hands move correctly throughout the swing – and your grip is fundamentally sound – you can be sure the clubface is in good position too. A simple and effective tip can help you monitor the movement of your hands. Take up your normal address position, but hold a dinner plate between your hands instead of a club.

2 ANGLE POISE
From the moment the swing starts your hands, arms and the plate should form identical angles. Your hands are forced to operate in unison which encourages a one piece takeaway. Halfway back the plate is in a vertical position with the edge pointing straight down the line. Note how the position of your left hand in relation to the plate is the same as at address – this should also be the case with a club in your hands.

There are two basic types of swing plane – upright and rounded. The style that shapes your swing depends a great deal on your height and build.

If you're tall, your swing plane is likely to be quite upright – like Greg Norman for example. If you're short and stocky, it's natural for your swing plane to be slightly rounder – in the style of Ian Woosnam.

There's no right or wrong swing plane, but you must have a style that works for you time and time again. Consistency is the most important factor.

CLASSIC UPRIGHT

Used by just about every classic swinger of the club, the upright swing looks stylish and elegant. Tom Weiskopf and Johnny Miller are perfect examples – their swings have been the envy of club golfers all over the world.

The hallmarks of an upright swing plane are high hands at the top of the backswing and a classic followthrough position. The clubhead stays more down the line throughout the swing. It's a style dominated by the left side and relies a great deal on strong hands and arms.

Many golfers who succeed with this type of swing tend to adopt a slow, rhythmical tempo. While you should always swing the club at your own pace, on an upright plane it's particularly important you give yourself time to be aware of the position of the clubhead.

Timing has to be spot on if you're to strike the ball consistently well from a high position at the top. The clubhead travels very much up and down – the margin for error is slim and any slight faults tend to be exaggerated.

An upright swing can also put a strain on the back. Many players in the past have flattened their swings to ease lower back problems – Seve Ballesteros and Jack Nicklaus are classic examples. The changes were small but nevertheless had a significant effect.

ROUND THE BODY

When you swing on a rounded plane the arms move around the body, rather than up and down on an upright plane. This is probably the most commonly used swing plane of the two main types.

The clubhead arrives at the ball

4 RETURN TO SQUARE
On the downswing the plate should return to square at impact with the back of your left hand facing the target – exactly the same position as at address. Translated on to the course this exercise can help you deliver the clubface square to the back of the ball. Although it looks strange, this drill has it's advantages – you can practise just about anywhere. And because a plate is much bigger than a clubface, it's easier to spot the difference between right and wrong.

3 MIRROR IMAGES
At the top of the backswing a comparison with a shot on the course shows clearly that the angle of the plate and the clubface is identical. If you achieve this position you can be certain that your swing is on plane. A full shoulder turn takes place and the right hand is in perfect position – underneath the plate providing the same support as though it were a club.

HOGAN'S PANE OF GLASS

Ben Hogan's single minded attitude to practice was arguably greater than that of any other golfer in history. Hogan was also the master technician. His description of the swing plane is probably the clearest of all.

Visualize a pane of glass resting from the ground to your shoulders at address – this is your swing plane and it should remain constant throughout the stroke. As your arms reach hip level on the takeaway they should be moving parallel to the glass and should remain parallel all the way to the top of the backswing.

It's easy to identify any faults. If you lift your arms you break the glass and if you swing too flat your arms move away from parallel. Both moves mean your swing is out of plane on the backswing which is likely to cause problems coming down.

On the downswing your arms and the clubhead remain below the level of the glass all the way through impact. The clubhead attacks the ball from the inside, reaches square at impact, and then travels inside the line on the way through. If you're on the wrong plane on the downswing, the glass is shattered along with the shot.

IMAGINARY PANE OF GLASS REPRESENTS PERFECT SWING PLANE

ARMS AND CLUBHEAD REMAIN BELOW LEVEL OF GLASS THROUGHOUT SWING

ROUND VERSUS UPRIGHT

ROUNDED SWING
While there are certain fundamentals to the swing, a close look at two experts with contrasting swing planes goes to prove that golf is very much an individual game.

At 5ft 9in (1.77m), Australian professional Wayne Grady is a fraction below average height for a golfer and solidly built. Both factors are conducive to swinging the club on a slightly more rounded plane than standard. Note the position of Grady's hands in relation to his right shoulder at the top of the backswing.

This is generally regarded as the sort of swing that breeds consistency. If you're built in the Wayne Grady mould, a rounded swing is likely to suit you perfectly.

HIGH HANDS
Fellow countryman Brett Ogle is built differently to Wayne Grady. As a result their swings contrast dramatically. At over 6ft 2in (1.86m) and less than 11 stone (70kg), Ogle is tall, slim and extremely supple.

His height allows him to swing comfortably on a very upright plane. Ogle takes the club back on a wide arc – combined with a high hand position at the top this means he can generate the enormous power which makes him one of the biggest hitters on the European Tour.

Timing needs to be spot on when your swing plane is very upright. For most club golfers the position achieved by Ogle is probably too high to achieve consistency – on an off day you may see the ball flying all over the course.

Flattened plane

A rounded swing plane is fine, but if the club starts to become laid off at the top – pointing way left of target – the effects can be disastrous.

Halfway through the backswing the shaft of the club should point directly at the ball (see dotted line). But if the arms move around the body too much the club is set on an extremely flat plane (see solid line).

At the top of the backswing the club is clearly laid off. The hands are too flat and the left arm is almost horizontal. From this position the club is destined to strike the ball from way inside the line – a big hook or push tends to be the result.

on a shallow angle of attack – this helps produce a lower trajectory shot and a more consistent squaring of the clubface to the ball at impact. It's generally easier to draw the ball if your swing is round rather than upright.

While you can strike a ball equally well with an upright or round swing, the slightly flatter technique is widely thought to produce more consistent results – particularly under intense pressure.

Modern teaching methods tend to sway in favour of the rounded swing. Nick Faldo and Howard Clark are two well publicized examples of successful golfers who remodelled their swings.

But very few club golfers have the time, dedication or ability to carry out a complete rebuild job on their swings.

For this reason alone it's essential to have a swing plane that suits your physique – this is the style that is most likely to work for you and yield the best results from one week to the next.

FLATTEN AN UPRIGHT SWING

1 HONE YOUR ADDRESS

A very upright swing has a tendency to make you swing across the line from out to in and also places enormous importance on perfect timing. If you want to make your swing plane more rounded, the answer lies in the first part of your backswing. First make sure your address position is sound. Lie a club on the ground parallel to the ball-to-target line – this is an excellent visual aid to help you align correctly.

2 START ON PLANE

Take the club back fractionally inside the line and low to the ground. Concentrate on keeping your left arm and the shaft of the club in one piece to help generate a wide arc on the backswing. This pulls your shoulders, upper body and hips in unison – it also sets the club on a more rounded plane from the moment the swing starts.

SPOT THE DIFFERENCE

PATH OR PLANE?

Swing path is often confused with swing plane. While one does have an influence over the other, it's essential to be aware of the fundamental difference.

The best way to understand swing path is to imagine the clubhead as the only moving part in your swing that matters. The direction of the clubhead – particularly important through impact – is your individual swing path. In-to-in is the path you should always strive to achieve. In-to-out and out-to-in are faults that need correcting.

Swing path is influenced by swing plane – the angle the clubhead moves on in relation to the ground. A flat, rounded swing tends to deliver the clubhead to the ball on an in-to-out path. An upright swing is prone to causing an out-to-in swing path.